HIGHER ALTITUDES

Life Lessons Learnt at 35,000 ft

Joanne Harte

Foreword by **Rev. Louis Crawford**

Higher Altitudes: Lessons Learned at 35,000 ft.

Copyright © 2019 by Joanne Harte

All rights reserved. No part of this document may be reproduced or transmitted in any form, by any means (electronic, photocopying, recording, or otherwise) without the written permission of the author.

Scriptures marked AMP are taken from the AMPLIFIED BIBLE (AMP): Scripture taken from the AMPLIFIED® BIBLE, Copyright © 1954, 1958, 1962, 1964, 1965, 1987 by the Lockman Foundation Used by Permission. (www.Lockman.org)

Scriptures marked GNB are taken from the GOOD NEWS BIBLE (GNB): Scriptures taken from the Good News Bible© 1994 published by the Bible Societies/HarperCollins Publishers Ltd UK, Good News Bible© American Bible Society 1966, 1971, 1976, 1992. Used with permission.

Scriptures marked KJV are taken from the KING JAMES VERSION (KJV): KING JAMES VERSION, public domain.

Scriptures marked NIV are taken from the NEW INTERNATIONAL VERSION (NIV): Scripture taken from THE HOLY BIBLE, NEW INTERNATIONAL VERSION ®. Copyright© 1973, 1978, 1984, 2011 by Biblica, Inc.™. Used by permission of Zondervan

Scriptures marked NKJV are taken from the NEW KING JAMES VERSION (NKJV): Scripture taken from the NEW KING JAMES VERSION®. Copyright© 1982 by Thomas Nelson, Inc. Used by permission. All rights reserved

Scripture quotations marked (NLT) are taken from the Holy Bible, New Living Translation, copyright © 1996, 2004, 2007, 2013, 2015 by Tyndale House Foundation. Used by permission of Tyndale House Publishers, Inc., Carol Stream, Illinois 60188. All rights reserved.

This book is affectionately dedicated to the Lewis and Harte families

I am happy God blessed me with you all.

ACKNOWLEGEMENTS

It is truly a blessing to have the support of my family and friends. I am grateful to God for all the help that came my way.

I wish to express sincere gratitude to Rev. Louis Crawford, Senior Pastor of Tucville House of Prayer, in Georgetown Guyana. Thank you for agreeing to write the Foreword for this project. You have been my shepherd and father down through the decades. I appreciate you.

To my now Pastor and First Lady, Rev. Trevor Parris and Lady Jewel Parris, a heartfelt gratitude. You have been such a great blessing to me. I thank God for your ministry and friendship.

To my precious brother and friend, Rev. Rudolph Prescod, I have been blessed to have known you since my young adult age, and you are still here. Thank you for being there for me. I really do appreciate you.

Higher Altitudes: Lessons Learned at 35,000 ft.

Contents

ACKNOWLEGEMENTS 4
Contents 6
FOREWORD 7
INTRODUCTION 8
LESSON#1 10
    SCENARIO#1 11
Lesson#2 20
    SCENARIO#2 21
LESSON#3 29
    SCENARIO#3 30
LESSON#4 39
    SCENARIO#4 40
LESSON#5 49
    SCENARIO#5 50
LESSON#6 60
    SCENARIO#6 61
LESSON#7 71
    SCENARIO#7 72
    THEDE-BRIEFING 81
IN THE 86
FINAL ANALYSIS 87
NOTES 94
About the Author 97

FOREWORD

God answers prayers, and because He does we are encouraged so to do, often, and in various ways.

The Lord has His protocol for answered prayer which often times we adhere to unknowingly and He answers.

Air travel is one of those ventures we engage in without being aware of the various procedures necessary to complete the journey.

Joanne has used her experience in the Aviation Arena to draw parallels from that perspective to God's protocol for prayer, as a result giving us a fresh insight into this ministry.

From this work, we benefit in at least two ways:

- o The protocol of praying successfully

- o An understanding of all that it entails in an airline trip

His disciples saw Jesus praying and they asked Him to teach them to pray. They realized that they needed to know something more about prayer. Joanne considers some of the underlining truths about what is necessary for fruitful praying.

Having been involved in the Aviation Industry for more than thirty (30) years; her application is both inspiring and refreshing.

You cannot help but be blessed and encouraged to persevere in seeking the Lord. PRAY

Rev. Louis Crawford
Senior Pastor, House of Prayer – Tucville, Guyana
Former Chief Pilot – Guyana Airways Corporation

INTRODUCTION

It was sometime during my pre-teen years that I came across this magazine. It was a KLM newsletter of some sort. The cover caught my eyes. It was a lovely picture of a smiling Flight Attendant offering a meal to a passenger who seemed happy to be on board that aircraft.

The tray filled with what I know now to be plastic disposable utensils, seemed to have the best assortment of delicious items my eyes had ever seen. I particularly fell in love with the presentation of the butter [yes butter];it was a little teaspoon size spread delicately shaped in the form of a rose.

This cover photograph had an impact on me; so much so, that it was then that I decided in my head that I wanted to become a Flight Attendant. I guess that was my first encounter with what everyone now calls a 'vision-board' or 'dream-board.'

I envisioned myself in service to nice people. Back in those days, everyone was very delightful, courteous, and decent. I wanted to be one of those who would serve the delightful,courteous decent passengers on-board.

This vision stayed with me. In fact, in retrospect, I had seen myself on-board an aircraft daily. I spoke of it to my childhood friends. It was ingrained in my heart.

When I became a teenager, I remember asking my mother to make me a skirt suit that resembled the uniform of an airline that existed at the time – Guy-America. She did it so well, and I was so satisfied.I would wear this 'uniform' to church with every opportunity I got. It was my favorite thing to wear. I even went to the airline office dressed in that uniform to submit my application for the position. Of course, I didn't get the job, but that did not kill my hopes.

The Word of God is so true – if we can believe it we shall receive it; we will have what we decree.

> Proverbs 18:21 says, *"Death and life are in the power of the tongue; and they that love it shall eat the fruit thereof"*(KJV).

Fast forwarding! It's been several decades now since I've been serving in the airline industry. I started as a teenager, and I am still going at it. I met some interesting people, some delightful and some not quite so. I have also visited some exotic places. The industry has been good to me; I have no regrets. It has been lots of fun travelling. However, the time is quickly coming for me to transition out of this and prepare for the next level and dimension of my life. It is time to level UP!

I practically grew up in the airline industry. I made some mistakes but learnt lots of lessons. Those lessons learnt will be with me for the rest of my long life. These are some of the lessons I wish to share with you who were kind and caring enough to purchase and read this book.

Allow me to share seven (7) of the lessons I have learnt. Of course, there are many others, but THESE are really good principles to live by. Apply them, and they will serve you well.

They have worked and still do work well for me. I'm sure that they will also work well for you.

Be blessed as you digest.

Joanne

LESSON#1

First things first.
Seek Him out before we set out!

KEY NOTES

- Getting good Godly guidance before-hand gives us an advantage.

- Following those guidelines and instructions makes the process so much easier.

SCENARIO#1

The Briefing

As a Flight Attendant, it's just the norm that the first thing done whenever we report for duty, is to be gathered together as a crew by the captain for a briefing. Any special instructions, any known situations or anticipated challenges, are discussed in the briefing.

If there were any special passengers or celebrities expected, any high profile dignitaries booked and checked in for travel, this is the time all things are brought to the forefront.

The crew members are allowed to ask questions, get clarifications, and give suggestions, all in order that the trip be as stress free as possible.

The Lead Flight Attendant is required to ask for a briefing if the captain, for any reason, does not initiate it. Everything the crew needs to know would be divulged. Everyone is required to be in sync and on the same page. Manuals and announcements are sometimes checked to make sure that no one has missing bulletins, revisions, or updates. We would even find out what meals there are for the crew if it is a flight that caters crew dinners.

On the other hand, the traveling customers receive a briefing whenever they check in at the airport. They are informed of their flight number, seat number, time to board, boarding gates and everything they need to know before they get on that aircraft.

As things are in the natural realm, so they are in the spiritual realm.

Truth be told – the Bible says:

"But seek ye first the kingdom of God, and his righteousness, and all these things shall be added unto you"
Matthew 6:33(KJV).

"In all your ways acknowledge Him, and He shall direct your paths"
Proverbs 3:6 (NKJV).

The fact of the matter is

- If we would take the time to talk to and check in with the Lord God Almighty first thing at the start of our day;

- If we would allow Him to take the lead and to guide us;

- If we would initiate the conversation and communication;

- If we were to wait on Him for His suggestions and clarifications;

- If we would just make it a habit to seek Him out early before any other persons begin to speak in our ears, *[man I tell you]*, we certainly would not run into all the snags we find ourselves in as the day progresses. We will save ourselves a mountain of trouble and frustration. After all, He, Christ, is our Captain in Command. The Holy Spirit is our Chief Pilot. He's so much more than that too. He is also our Consultant in Chief, our Senior Partner, and our ever-present advocate. He is the one who knows all things, sees all things and has power over everything. This is the kind of person I want to have in my corner early in the morning, late at night and all day every day. This is the One I want whispering in my ear first thing as I open my eyes, and last thing at night.

- Let me honest with you. I have had days when I would be running late; those days when I would just be in a hurry to get to where I have to go – when I would just mumble a quick prayer under my breath and not take the time to seek His face in a more intimate way. And oh boy! Those were exactly the days I would be most fatigued and stressed. It's like my time wasn't being managed properly. I was doing so much work but accomplishing very little, pressure was high and my productivity low.I was planting much but harvesting little. After taking a close look and analyzing those days, I was able to trace my being overwhelmed to my lack of Quality Time (QT) with my *personal private Captain*; I missed the 'Briefing.'

- These days I've made it a necessity to pray. Midnight works well for me. I'm still up at that time, and the rest of the family is asleep. This time was just ideal. I can quietly concentrate – no phones are ringing, no one watching television, it's just so peaceful at that time.

- Listen, you don't have to take it from me, but try it for yourself. If you are one who finds that you need help to think more clearly and manage your activities and time in a better way, make it a priority to take time to pray and commune with Jesus before you start your day. Try it for at least twelve (12) minutes for twelve (12) days, then talk to me. You will see what a difference it makes in the outcome of your day.

- Prayer is powerful, it enriches our lives. I'm sure if you are a praying person, you can testify that praying helps; it keeps us going strong holistically. It is the necessary fuel needed for the 'fight' and for this 'flight' called life. Prayer, communicating with God first is the necessary Briefing.

- I have found that this *modus operandi* gives such clarity of thought and peace of mind. It opens up a whole new sense of calmness and the presence of prevailing peace. You and I both know that we need to keep our cool to navigate our way in the streets, in the marketplace, and in life generally. You have to have your head on straight. Seeking God first in prayer, in the Briefing, works better than anything else I know.

LIFE LONG LESSON LEARNT?

First things first!
Seek Him out before we set out!

So what will it be?

Take the time now to reflect on your own life. Please answer the following questions before you move on.

1. What is the very first thing you do before you start your day?

2. How does this first action affect your attitude?

3. What effect does your attitude have on the rest of your day?

4. How do you think praying first would make a difference in your day?

5. Why do you think it is worth your while spending the first twelve (12) minutes in prayer and meditation of the Word?

So let's do this!

Before we launch into our day, let's be sure to thank God for waking us up and for gifting us with another day of life. Be careful to ask for and embrace His guidance – the Briefing - throughout the day ahead. If we have a family, as much as possible, practice praying as a unit before heading out the doors.

We have all heard the phrase 'the family that prays together stays together.' Prayer unites families. If you are single, prayer still works, and prayer grounds us. There's something that happens in the atmosphere when a prayer leaves our mouth for God's ears. The Bible says,

> *"The effectual fervent prayer of the righteous man avails much"* (James 5:16)

Let us get our briefing and guidance from our Chief Pilot – Jesus Christ. He makes all the difference. Our consistent communication with Him will make a world

Let's pray!

Good morning Heavenly Father. Thank you for allowing me to see this brand new day. Thank you for another opportunity to experience your brand new mercies on today. I ask for your guidance in everything, your grace for everything and may your glory be seen in everything; everything I do, say and think. Help me to keep my mind stayed on you. I trust you with my life Father and thank you, in Jesus' name. Amen.

Higher Altitudes: Lessons Learned at 35,000 ft.

Lesson#2

He knows the way, Therefore, we follow His leadership

KEY NOTES:

- We save ourselves time and energy when we follow the One who created the way.

- Effectively playing our part on the team benefits not only us but also everyone around us.

SCENARIO #2

The Captain and Crew

The Captain, as we well know, is always the one in charge of the ship, whether it be an aircraft or a marine vessel, he or she is tasked with setting the tone for the rest of the crew. He gives the orders, and the team follows through.

The Captain is the one whose experience and expertise is superior to those in the rest of the crew, and rightfully so. After all, the Captain has been tested, tried and proven. He or she has put in their years and hours on the job, and might I add, survived it all.

The 'Miracle on the Hudson' was possible because an experienced Captain Chelsey 'Sully" Sullenberger was able to think clearly. He knew that his actions and decisions were either going to take or save lots of lives. He was positioned at the front end of the vessel, seeing what was ahead of him, and had all the facts needed to make an informed decision for himself and for those who were wholly dependent on him.

Southwest Airlines Captain Tammie Jo Shults whose aircraft suffered an engine failure in April 2018, knew she had to make quick decisions in order to avoid fatalities. Her ability to make prompt decisions would affect every passenger and every crew-member on that flight. Sadly, one life was lost, and that was painful. However, everyone else aboard that aircraft made it out alive and unharmed. Like Captain Sully, she had all the information, saw ahead, was knowledgeable of the possible outcomes, and made the quick evaluation for the best possible end result.

A good captain knows their craft, has spent countless hours in the simulator, yet no simulator can prepare anyone for all the possible scenarios out there.

What helps the smooth operation of any flight is the experience of the captain, and the respect he or she earns from their crew. A good Captain will earn the trust of those under his or her authority.

As it is in the natural realm, so is it in the spiritual realm.

Truth be told – the Bible says:

Where there is no [wise, intelligent] guidance, the people fall [and go off course like a ship without a helm], But in the abundance of [wise and godly] counselors there is victory.
Proverbs 11:14 (Amplified Bible)

The fact of the matter is

We have the best ever Captain in God our Heavenly Father. The kind of Captain who even though He always has the final say, is always right and is always right on time, yet allows us the freedom of choice in our decision-making. He is not one to force Himself and His principles on us. He invites us to be willing participants in this relationship of 'Captain and Crew.'

When the Captain takes over a ship, there are certain things he has to do. In fact, there are things he must do, in order to ensure safe operations.

Like in any other industry that runs efficiently and effectively, there are Standard Operating Procedures, what we call S.O.Ps. These are the set standards, regulations and policies that must be adhered to in order for the end result to be what it must be.

Before any flight takes to the sky, there are checks and balances along the way that must be carried out. The Engineer must do his part, the Fueling Technician must do his, Security must do theirs, the Dispatcher, the Air Traffic Controller, the Flight Attendants, First Officer, and Captain must all perform their functions in the most professional and thorough way to prevent mishaps. If one person along the chain fails to conduct his part without regard, things can get messy along the way.

Expert studies have shown that the biggest factor in airplane crashes is human error. Someone along the way failed to accurately and efficiently perform their duties, missing vital details. These check-lists must be gone over thoroughly every time a crew shows up for duty. This is the Standard Operating Procedures. If everything is not checked through and checked off, somebody or something down line will check out, and without warning; suddenly and maybe without remedy. Lives depend on us. The Captain has the final say as to whether or not he deems the aircraft fit for flight.

Our Supreme Captain, the Lord of Hosts, has provided a gift for us in the Holy Bible; the scriptures are our Standard Operating Procedures (S.O.Ps). Our lives go the way they sometimes do because we do not adhere to the S.O.Ps or because someone we are associated with failed to comply with the S.O.Ps. These guidelines were given to save us from ourselves. It's simple, know the instructions, follow the instructions and survive the impact (whatever life throws at us).

The Captain we have, the Lord God Almighty, sees all things, knows all things and can do all things, yet the stubborn *crewmembers* that we are, we cause our 'flight' to our destination to go in every other direction than straight ahead. It is high time we 'straighten up to fly right.' We must heed the instructions of our Captain in command.

What I love about the Lord is that regardless of our dislocated attention, He is faithful to guide us back to where we should be. He is that kind of Captain that genuinely cares about the welfare and wellbeing of His 'crew and passengers.'

LIFE LONG LESSON LEARNT?

He knows the way, therefore we follow His leadership!

So what will it be?

1. Are you opened to being taught new lessons, or do you prefer to be in control always? Why?

2. Do you think there are things you could do better if you were given good guidance/mentorship?

3. If your answer is yes, what are those things you could do better to enhance your life?

4. What's preventing you from changing this negative habit/s?

5. Explain why you think you are worth the effort of intentionally replacing negative attributes with positive ones.

So let's do this!

Following the instructions of 'The Captain,' who has the know-all, is just the logical thing, in fact, it is just the right thing to do. The instructions we followdetermine the decisions we make, and the decisions we make determine the life we have. When we follow the 'flight plan' and the S.O.Ps, our obedience will get us to where we need to go and will get us there safely. We are the crewmembers, let us adhere to the instructions of The Captain.

2 Timothy 3:16-17 says,

> *[16]All Scripture is given by inspiration of God, and is profitable for doctrine, for reproof, for correction, for instruction in righteousness, [17]that the man of God may be complete, thoroughly equipped for every good work.* (KJV)

The Holy Bible is our manual. Scriptures are given to us for everyday practical living. Its principles, when applied, lead to an abundant life.

Study and meditate on the Word of God daily. Put it into practice. The Word of God is alive and gives freshness to life. The Word of God is the will of God for us. Let us pray the Word over our lives, and over the lives of our loved ones.

Here is a good SOS formula for success.

S – Study diligently [meditate daily]
O – Obey always [practice consistently]
S – Soar higher[survive every challenge]

The Word is the *Captain's* instructions to us.
Let's pray!

Heavenly Father, I come before you in the name of Jesus. I thank you for your Word that is a lamp to my feet and a light to my path. As I meditate on your Word and promises to me today, help me to hide this Word in my heart so that it will keep me from falling in times of challenges. In everything, let me not lean on my own understanding, but rather listen to the prompting of your Holy Spirit – that still small voice. Thank you for speaking to me through your Word. I pray in no other name but the name of Jesus. Amen.

LESSON#3

Whatever WE do, WE should do it with all our strength and with all our heart as onto Him!

KEY NOTES:

- Let's give today's task our best shot; tomorrow we will be happy we did.

- What sometimes looks like a big setback oftentimes is a bigger setup for our biggest come back.

SCENARIO #3

The Assignment

Well, like we have discussed, and as you and I both know, the Captain is in command of all the crew on board. His assignment is to man the front end – making decisions for the rest of the *souls* on board the flight.

In the passenger cabin, the Lead Flight Attendant is the one in charge. The Lead is the one that assigns the positions to the rest of the cabin crew. Everyone has an assignment. Our assignment or our position dictates which part of the aircraft we will work, which area we will cover in the security search, which emergency exits fall under our purview if anything of that nature were to occur.

Sometimes, we are put in a position we are not too comfortable with, but we have to give it our best shot. After all, it is the vocation we signed up for.

Even though everyone receives the same training, everyone cannot be in the lead position. We all cannot be the Lead Flight Attendant. There is only room for one leader at a time.

When our assigned post is given to us, it defines the parameters within which we should perform our duties. Boundaries are set because they are necessary for the smooth flow of things. Who wants to dwell in an environment where the lines are always blurred? I certainly do not want to, and I think you wouldn't welcome such a situation either.

If we have the eagle mentality, if we want to go places, and want to soar higher, we will respect the leadership with the understanding that the only difference between our position and theirs, is that they have a greater level of responsibility. We will recognize that good followers make excellent leaders when their season for leadership comes around. Our attitude determines if we are fit for flying at Higher Altitudes.

As things are in the natural, so they parallel in the spiritual realm.

Truth be told - The Bible says:

[11] And he gave some, apostles; and some, prophets; and some, evangelists; and some, pastors and teachers;
[12] For the perfecting of the saints, for the work of the ministry, for the edifying of the body of Christ:
Ephesians 4:11-16 (KJV)

The fact of the matter is

If we learn how to be good followers, we will become exceptional leaders. It takes discipline to submit to authority – to hold our post – especially when there is something inside of us pushing and pulling for us to be and do more. We must acknowledge that to climb to leadership, it takes a process.

I remember like it was yesterday, even though it has been decades since, when I worked at Guyana Airways Corporation. A vacancy for the post of Flight Attendant Instructor became available. The vacancy was opened to all Flight Attendants.

Management had stated that they only needed one Instructor to fill the position. Out of all the Flight Attendants, only two of us submitted applications for consideration. The other Flight Attendant who applied had all the qualifications required for the post, while I did not. In fact, he had already had experience as an Instructor. We both were invited to the interviews. I walked in the room with my head held as high and left the room with the same confidence. Even though I knew that I started out at a disadvantage, I was just grateful that God allowed me to experience the interview.

When the results came back, management decided to promote us both. They decided on having two instructors instead of one as was originally planned.

Now having come up a tad bit short on my qualifications; having not been in that position before, meant that I had to dig deep to prove myself during the probation period. If I ever needed help, if I ever needed an angel, I needed one then.

Have you ever been in such a predicament? Ever felt like all the odds were stacked against you? Ever went head first into a new venture trusting and praying that by some miracle you'll get through the task with your skin still intact? Yes? It is heart-throbbing, and yes, miracles still do happen.

To this day I believe God answered my prayers. He blessed me with not only one but two angels. I will always hold them dear to my heart.

My friends Jennifer and Beverley took me under their wings. They mentored me into readiness for the assignment. Jennifer was the Department Director, and Beverley was a Senior Supervisor and Instructor. They worked hard with me; they worked tirelessly for me. I will always be grateful.

I said all that to say this, little did I know that that assignment was going to be the foundation and preparation for my *now assignment*. Practicing my instructor skills in front of an audience of familiar faces, most of whom had positioned themselves to be stumbling blocks, had become instead the stepping stone for me to become a well sought after Trainer and Presenter– my now assignment.

That assignment worked very well for me. I am still reaping the benefits of the hard work put in on that assignment.

LIFE LONG LESSON LEARNT?

Whatever we do, we do it with all our strength and with all our heart as onto Him!

So what will it be?

1. Name one thing you are required to do (at work, school or home) that you wish you didn't have to.

2. What about it do you find so undesirable and detesting?

3. What do you imagine would be the end result if you made a deliberate attempt to change your attitude regarding that assignment?

4. How can you master this task in the future?

5. List any other areas of your life in which your mastering this assignment may serve you well in the future.

So let's do this!

Regardless of where we are in our careers, our studies or our personal phase of life, though it may feel uncomfortable, let us learn to give the assignment our best shot. We will find later on that it would have served as a *setup* even though it felt like a *setback*.

We should cultivate an *attitude of gratitude* for the opportunity to serve, the ability to work and the capacity to love. Oftentimes, and especially in the initial stages of a new opportunity or venture, we are not entirely in a position to decide all the factors of and characters in the game. What we have control over is how we will play our part and the attitude we chose to adopt in the situation.

I am quite certain we have all heard it before:

Most of the time, it's our attitude, not our aptitude that determines our altitude.

Let us remember this: Philippians 1:6 says

> *He who began a good work in you, will be faithful to complete it until the day of Jesus Christ.*

2 Timothy 1:12 reminds us that….He is able to keep that which we commit to Him until the day of reckoning.

I would recommend that we look for and choose to learn the lessons from our every encounter. Somewhere down the road, we'll be happy we did.

Let's pray

My God and Heavenly Father, I come to you today in the name of Jesus Christ. I am thankful for the blessing you bestowed on me through my now assignment. Help me to serve wholeheartedly and with loyalty to those in assignment and authority over me. As I serve, allow me to be a blessing to everyone I come into contact with. May I always perform at my very best so that they will see You in me. Thank you for hearing and answering my prayer...in Jesus' name. Amen

LESSON#4

Our quality of life hinges on the quality of our relationship with Him and with those around us.

KEY NOTES:

- Fostering positive relationships affects our health and wellbeing in positive ways.

- We can make the world [our world] a better place with one hello or one smile at a time.

SCENARIO#4

Welcome Aboard

Good morning!

Welcome!

Good to see you again!

How are you today?

Love that hair!

It still gives me pleasure even after all these years, to stand at the forward entry door and greet every passenger coming onto the aircraft.

For the most part, I try to make eye contact with everyone. However, some folks are very shy. I can see them making every effort to not look at me fully. They'll give half a smile or none at all. I let them be.

In the Caribbean, we were cultured to say hello and good morning. We greeted everyone we met along the way. It's just the Caribbean warmth; just the way we did things.

I enjoy working with people. I still enjoy serving people. Some of my colleagues have labelled me as being *too* 'accommodating,' but that's me and I feel like that's the job.

This way of functioning in my professional life has translated to my personal life as well. It's just natural for me. Whenever we go out as a family, my brother always reminds me that I'm not at work. We would be in the restaurant, and I'd be tidying up.

I am not afraid to serve. I see it as helping someone else to become better at what they do. We never know what the other person is dealing with in their private life, or even on their jobs, and sometimes, just sometimes, going the extra mile helps.

I remember flying from Dallas to New York one evening. An elderly lady was flying as a non-revenue passenger. She was so happy just to be on the flight without a hassle.

She happened to have a first-class seat, and that section was my responsibility. I offered the meal and beverage service, cleared the utensils and offered another round of beverages. All during this time, I noticed her looking at me a little differently. You know that look? I am quite sure you know when someone is looking at you in a kind of way that says *'can we talk for a minute?'* So I stopped by her seat to say hello – and that's all she wanted.

The gist of the story is that she had always flown with her husband by her side. He was deceased for over ten (10) years, and this was the first time she was flying any airline since. She was emotional but my listening ear alleviated some of her fears and calmed her nerves. Just listening helped to make her day a bit better. She felt valued and welcomed.

And as it is in the natural realm, so it is found in the realm of the spirit.

Truth be told – the Bible says:

Do not neglect to extend hospitality to strangers [especially among the family of believers—being friendly, cordial, and gracious, sharing the comforts of your home and doing your part generously], for by this some have entertained angels without knowing it.
Hebrews 13:2 (Amplified Bible)

The fact of the matter is

We were created for social interaction. To talk, to laugh and to love is just natural. That's how God designed us. Like Himself, He made us for connecting with others. We were made for fellowship. That's why we don't have to teach a baby how to give a smile to the person their eyes connect with. It's just instinctive.

In this social-media dispensation, it seems, however, like we place more emphasis on the *media* than we do on the *social* aspect. This lack of social skills or more so, the lack of intentional person to person socializing, is what causes our young ones to become withdrawn, introverted and angry to the point of bitterness – hating everyone who is different in behavior or belief. As adults, we are guilty sometimes of not paying as much attention to our young people as we ought to. This results in them developing feelings of rejection, harboring hurt and resentment. In the final analysis, we leave room for diabolical influences to invade and infect their souls [the seat of their minds, emotions, and will]and their spirits.

In a world where we seem to have become so disconnected and anti-social; where we are more into gadgets than friendly gatherings, we fail to see that the breakdown in our society is as a result of the breakdown in our human nexus. Our blatant disregard and disrespect for each other has caused us to cultivate the highest level of devaluation on life, more than we have ever experienced as a species, and sadly so.

Do you know anyone who resembles and displays the tendencies of a loner? We all know someone who prefers to be alone – be by themselves with themselves, but it's not good that any man [mankind] be alone. Of course, there are those times that we need solitude for our own sanctity, but to be alone all the time, is certainly not healthy.

LIFE LONG LESSON LEARNT?

The quality of our lives hinges on the quality of our relationship with Him and with those around us.

So what will it be?

1. How many of the persons on your facebook page do you know personally? How often do you interact one-on-one with them?

2. When was the last time you called or visited with a relative or friend that you haven't seen in a long time? How long did your conversation last?

3. How would it affect your relationship with your family members if you were to have deliberately planned dinners together; where no one brought their cell phones to the table, but rather engaged in wholesome conversations?

4. What effects would it have on your outlook on life were you to intentionally befriend that one person you recognize who struggles with connecting to people?

5. List three (3) things you can imagine would take place in your environment were you to purposefully say hello and smile with the neighbors, co-workers and the people at church?

So let's do this

Let's take the time to reach out to people, our neighbors, folk we see every day and even those we do not see often. To that person who wants nothing to do with anyone, say hello, give a quick smile, as much as they will allow you to get in. Do it consistently. They think they don't but they do need the interaction for their own mental stability, and we – we can make a difference in their life.

I am precious. You are precious. We are all precious. People are priceless; we are of highest value to God. We shouldn't allow anyone to tell us or treat us otherwise. To God, everyone matters!

I have come to understand that regardless of who and how they are, we do not have to be scared to welcome a new acquaintance. My suggestion to us is this, let us not be ever afraid to create new friendships. Relationships serve a purpose. Whether they be for a reason or just for a season, good relationships are valuable. Let's cherish our good connections. Let us seek to foster better friendships, not just because we think that they may work for our benefit sometime in the future, and they very well might we never know, but because we have something to offer to the next person. We can offer a smile or cheerful hello. Every tiny gesture of friendliness makes a difference. It makes a difference in us, it makes a difference in the world around us. It does so much for us when you learn that our lives are not only about us, but we were purposed to leave our mark on this earth before we go. It enhances our soul; gives us great peace when we come to the matured consciousness that our own lives are so much more enriched when we lend of ourselves to others.

Relationships at work, at church and at home need to be fostered. We need to nurture those relationships that are healthy for us. At the same token, we should as much as possible, avoid toxic and diabolic connections. They come only to trap us and drain us of our energy. Rather we should seek to invest in solid, trustworthy friendships. They do make a world of difference. Good friendships and relationships give great returns on our investments.

We should intentionally welcome new positive relationships aboard our lives.

Let's pray

Father in Heaven, I love you. I thank you for my family and friends; for those you have put in my path. Help me to seek to be a blessing to all I come into contact with. Let me take no one for granted but display in a way that glorifies you, love, compassion and genuine kindness. Let me not be afraid to be my brothers' keeper. I desire to fortify those relationships that enhance my life and walk with you, show me how. From today, I seek to make a difference in my corner, and may this love and care be contagious. I pray in no other name but the name of Jesus Christ my Lord. Amen.

LESSON #5

All things indeed work together for good, to those of us who love the Lord and are called according to His purpose for our lives

KEY NOTES:

- Not because *it's* not going good for us right now means that *it's* not going to be good for us later on.

- Life has a way of working things out and worrying contributes absolutely nothing positive to the end result.

SCENARIO#5

Prepare for Departure

Manydays, flying out of New York's LaGuardia is challenging. Dealing with the construction of the airport, the traffic, crowd flow and that is all before you even get to the security check point. If you happen to be using public transportation, I would strongly recommend you leave home at least four hours before you need to be there or things could get messy.

On the tarmac, the stress often continues. From bird strikes to workers' strikes. It is hectic. The delays can get outrageous in the New York City air space. Flying out of New York, we have to 'prepare [our minds] for departure' - a long departure.

Returning to the gate after sitting on the tarmac for several hours, is not unheard of. It's not at all unusual. The tarmac delay program gets used quite frequently at LaGuardia, especially in the winter months. Regulations require that after being off the gate with passengers on board for three hours, we must return to the terminal, disembark and reset the clock. Sometimes we get back on the runway to wait another few hours again before taking off.

One would hope this didn't happen too often but on time departures rarely occur in the New York area at peak time. As a result, people miss their connections and their meetings. They become angry and agitated, and in most cases, these inconveniences are beyond the control of the airlines. It is just the way things are in such a congested air space.

I recall not so long ago, we were on a three-day trip that the captain referred to as 'a trip from hell.' Every day, in fact, every leg of every day, we faced challenges. There were severe thunder storms in the neighborhood which caused tarmac delays, detours, cancellations, re-assignments – all this 'excitement' was just too much for one trip. It seemed like the storms followed us everywhere. We encountered storms literally at every destination which resulted in further delays.

Passengers got anxious and irritated; the crew got tired and hungry; thank God for Jesus who gave me a song in my spirit – because that's what kept me going. It seemed like everything was stacked against us as we prepared for departure.

These natural inconveniences can often be paralleled in our spiritual life as well.

> ## Truth be told – the Bible says:
>
> *But in that coming day, no weapon turned against you will succeed. You will silence every voice raised up to accuse you. These benefits are enjoyed by the servants of the LORD; their vindication will come from me. I, the LORD, have spoken!*
> Isaiah 54:17(NLT)

The fact of the matter is

That's exactly how life pans out sometimes. Have you or anyone you know ever been caught in a situation where everything seemed to be working against you? Wherever you turned, it seemed like you would hit a brick wall. It looked like someone, or something had it out for you. I have been in those kinds of circumstances a few times. In fact, being honest with ourselves, most of us have been in such or a similar scenario. Whether it was in our career, in our finances, in our marriage or just in life generally, we have had to deal with a few challenges we didn't care for nor cater for.

However, I have found that it is in these kind of crisis situations that we grow by leaps and bounds. Challenges serve their purpose. One of the purposes is to *push* us to our *purpose* – our calling.

Tests and trials were made for overcoming. Opposition builds resilience. Resilience leads to strength of character.

Sometimes when we face persecutions and trials, we feel as if no one else can understand what we are going through. It feels as if we have the biggest problem ever. However, if we were to ask Job for his take on things, we might very well come to appreciate that life could be a whole lot worse – it is not as bad as it seems.

In Job's case, he suffered tremendously. Every weapon we can think of seemed to have been fashioned against him, but that's not the end of his story. He prayed – prayed for his friends and those who pretended to be his friends. The end result? He was triumphant — what a glorious victory! God rewarded him with double for his trouble. He refused to allow his pain to preclude him from walking in his purpose.

> **LIFE LONG LESSON LEARNT?**
>
> All things indeed work together for good, to those of us who love the Lord and are called according to His purpose for our lives

So what will it be?

1. Let's be honest with ourselves. Describe your attitude, in times past, when things did not go exactly the way you planned?

2. How did your attitude/demeanor in that situation affect the outcome/end result of the circumstances? Wasit a positive or negative effect?

3. Explain how you think a positive rather than a negative outlook would affect you and the end result, if that or a similar situation were to occur again?

4. What are those things in you that you think you need to change in order not to allow life circumstances to get you frustrated to the point of giving up?

5. What advice would you give some person you see throwing a tantrum over their adverse state of affairs?

So let's do this

When things seem to be going against us, let's remember airplanes can take off against the wind.

Climbing is always going to take a bit more energy and effort from us when compared to our going downhill. It is important for us to be prepared for our take off and ascent.

With all the traps our enemy has put in place to keep us stagnated; when we consider all the disruptions, distractions and diversions that could take place on a daily basis, we have to intentionally cultivate a mindset for moving forward. We must let nothing stop us. We must allow no one to kill our momentum. We were designed to be unstoppable.

I came across this quote one day in the classroom at Bible Institute. It's really excellent.

"I didn't come here to be average, I came to be awesome!"

Read it again. This time read it out loud enough so you can hear yourself.

"I didn't come here to be average, I came to be awesome!"

Read it out loud one more time – this time with attitude, declare it to the world:

"I didn't come here to be average, I came to be awesome!"

I love it! I love it! I love it! It is energizing.

Anytime we feel 'average' trying to creep up on us, just let us remind ourselves, we didn't come this far, we didn't do this much, we certainly didn't go through all that we have been through to be average. We are awesome in and through Christ.

Our enemies, those who try to hinder our climb, spiritually or otherwise, will be left with their mouths open. We are the head and not the tail. By divine design, we were meant to be above and not beneath. We are awesome in Christ.

I believe in my heart of hearts that that is how our Creator – Almighty God – meant for us to be. We were made in His image and likeness. We have His DNA, and He is *awesome to the max!*

Christ would never encourage us to imitate Him if He didn't give us the capacity to do so. He has always been *unstoppable and unshakable,* and with His help, we too can become.

We must accept that there are things we cannot control. Let us quit fussing about those things. The things we have control over, when the time comes, we must take the bull by the horn.

If we are determined to live to our fullest, if we even as much as think we were created for more, then we must condition ourselves and position ourselves to do whatever we have to do to prepare and be ready for our Higher Altitude.

Come up Higher is His call to us all.

We can do all things with the help of the One who is and gives us our strength.

To borrow from Bishop TD Jakes:-

Get ready, get ready, get ready!

Prepare for Departure.

Let's pray

Father in Heaven, thank you for the opportunity to start this new journey with you. Your Word says that promotion [spiritually, physically, emotionally, etc...] comes from you. As I prepare myself, mind, body, and spirit, allow me to recognize and walk through every open door you set before me. I press towards the mark of the high calling in you Christ Jesus. At the same time, help me to accept the truth, that for me, some doors are better off closed. In everything, I give you thanks. For you are my refuge and my strength and a present help in this and every season. Thank you for doing all things well. In Jesus name, I pray. Amen

LESSON #6

Knocked down does not have to mean knocked out!
With God on our side, we are winners.

KEY NOTES:

- Slips and falls happen, the important thing is that you get back up again.

- Do not allow yourself to become your own stumbling block.

SCENARIO #6

At Cruising Altitude

Now after liftoff, passing through the clouds, we come to expect some rumblings in the weather. We call it light chops. Then we come to that place where the plane settles down, and everything is going smoothly.

We offer the in-flight service and move around to make sure everyone is doing well. For a brief moment, we even forget we are flying because everything seems so calm; everything is moving alongeffortlessly. We're at cruising altitude.

All of a sudden, and without warning, the aircraft drops vehemently– a few feet down. Everyone screams. The captain comes on the public address system to say as calmly as he could, 'fasten your seat belts please.' He continues, 'Flight Attendants take your seats immediately.' Everyone, passengers and crew, scramble for their seats and seat belts. Before we could be buckled in properly, there comes another drop. Some call it 'air pocket.' It is Clear Air Turbulence, and we call it C.A.T.

Imagine having to deal with varying wind speeds at 35,000 feet. As we well know, storms have different degrees of intensity. In aviation, we classify the effects of these storms as light, moderate, severe and extreme turbulence. For the most parts, the radar is able to pick up these weather patterns so as to alert the Flight Deck as to what lies ahead. Sometimes this information comes from other aircraft flying in the vicinity. It always helps to be warned and made aware of the brewing weather around, but then there is C.A.T.

Clear Air Turbulence is the kind of disturbance that the radar does not detect. The Flight Deck cannot see it coming, therefore, the back end gets no warning. We just feel the impact, the jolt. We find out what is happening when it's already happened. The vessel ahead of us has no clue as to what has happened if they did not suffer its wrath.

A while back, we were flying into Cheddi Jagan International Airport, [GEO] Guyana from John F Kennedy [JFK] International. We were somewhere over the Caribbean Islands, about an hour and a half out of Timehri, when out of the clear blue skies, came this severe turbulent weather pattern. It would be my very first encounter with C.A.T. If you ever had one such incident, you will remember it for the rest of your life.

For quite a few weeks after that incident, I still had the lumps, bumps, and bruises as proof of the trauma. The pains eventually dissipated, the scars faded and I was back in business in no time - up and running, in fact up and flying, still to this day.

And as we all know by now [yes – say it with me], as things are in the natural, so they are paralleled in the spiritual world.

Truth be told - the Bible says:

The godly may trip seven times, but they will get up again. But one disaster is enough to overthrow the wicked.
Proverbs 24:16(NLT)

The fact of the matter is

That's life. Life throws us some curve balls when we least expect them, and there is nothing we can do circumvent them. Oftentimes we have no control over what is happening. The only thing we can control in such situations is our own actions; our own attitude. Whatever we decide to do, life continues. We get up, brush off and get going again. In most cases, we do not have the luxury of someone picking us up, we have to pick ourselves up. Our neighbor has his own strains and struggles to deal with. As recording artistes Donald Lawrence and The Tri-City Singers would put it:

> "Sometimes you have to encourage yourself.
> Sometimes you have to speak victory during the test.
> And no matter how you feel,
> Speak the word and you will be healed;
> Speak over yourself,
> Encourage yourself in the Lord."

Life happens! Our resilience and ability to make quick informed decisions get us through. We have to quickly decide to get up and get back in the game.

I have to confess, I've been knocked down a few times, but I also have recently cultivated a 'Terminator Mentality' – "I'll be back"…and if I can come back from those ordeals I have suffered, I believe anyone can come back from their ordeal. And not only come back but come back better; much stronger than when we were down on the ground.

I hear you! I hear you loud and clear. Your situation is harder; your circumstances are different. You're down on the ground and you can't seem to find your way back up on your feet. Guess what? I will never trivialize your tribulations. Not everyone can bounce back from the stuff you have gone through, but I believe you can, and in fact, I know that you will with the help of the Lord.

Absolutely, nothing is wrong with being knocked down. Where it becomes absurd is when we decide to give up, when we to stay down and allow the devil to count us out. It becomes even more absurd when we hand our power and authority over to that person or situation which caused us to be thrown off our feet in the first place.

My friend let me ask you this. What good will it serve to be counted out? What good will it do for those around us if we were to remain flat on the floor, refusing to help ourselves? If we need help, please let us get help. There is someone somewhere who is able and willing to help us overcome all the pain we have suffered.

The man in the Book of John Chapter 5, sat by the pool year after year, in fact, for thirty-eight (38) years to be exact, waiting for someone to come by to put him in the water. For thirty-eight (38) years – that is a very long time. That is a lot of time to lose.

John 5(NKJV)

> [1]*After this, there was a feast of the Jews, and Jesus went up to Jerusalem.*[2]*Now there is in Jerusalem by the Sheep Gate a pool, which is called in Hebrew, Bethesda, having five porches.*[3]*In these lay a great multitude of sick people, blind, lame, paralyzed, waiting for the moving of the water.*[4]*For an angel went down at a certain time into the pool and stirred up the water; then whoever stepped in first, after the stirring of the water, was made well of whatever disease he had.*[5]*Now a certain man was there who*

had an infirmity thirty-eight years. ⁶*When Jesus saw him lying there and knew that he already had been in that condition a long time, He said to him, "Do you want to be made well?"* ⁷*The sick man answered Him, "Sir, I have no man to put me into the pool when the water is stirred up; but while I am coming, another steps down before me."* ⁸*Jesus said to him, "Rise, take up your bed and walk."* ⁹*And immediately the man was made well, took up his bed, and walked.*

Were you ever in a position where you felt nothing or no one could help you? I have been there. And that is exactly the position this man found himself in, seated by the pool. We have all felt like we've been there, but some have allowed themselves to be stuck there.

I thank God for Jesus. Jesus passed by and rendered assistance. He made that man at the pool whole, and He is so ready to do the same for us all.

I have to say this. We are too precious, life is too valuable, and we are worth so much more. This is what Jesus said about us:

> *"Anyone who strikes you strikes what is most precious to me. So the LORD Almighty sent me with this message for the nations that had plundered his people."* Zechariah 2:8 (Good News Translation)

Almighty God sees us as so treasured and dear to Him. He thought we were worth dying for and He did exactly that, so we might have the amazingly abundant life He always intended for us to have.

Christ gave His life for us so that we would not have to give up our lives to anyone or anything else. Let us not allow the enemy to knock us down and count us out. Hey, let us get up and live.

LIFE LESSONS LEARNT?

Knocked down does not have to mean knocked out!
With God on our side, we are winners.

So what will it be?

1. Think back to that moment in time when that situation blind-sided you [that failed marriage or relationship, illness, loss of employment] and you thought there was no way out. Explain your thoughts and feelings at the time.

2. If you have moved forward already, examine how you got up and moved forward.

3. What did you learn about yourself and your level of resilience during that trial?

4. It's never about your tribulations, rather it's about your attitude during the tribulations. Do you see where you have it in you to overcome every test every time?

5. If no, examine what adjustments in your mindset need to made in order for you to be empowered to overcome every time.

So let's do this

Regardless of how hard a hit we took; how low to the bottom of the barrel we fell, know this, if we can look up, if we can imagine getting up, then we are half way there. This battle is in our mind.

The Word of God said that He is able to do exceeding abundantly above all **we** can ask or imagine, according to the power that works in **us**(Ephesians 3:20).

Stop for a while and read **Psalm 107**. Go ahead – read it now. Read it analytically. Take your time. I promise you the rest of this book will be right here when you come back.

Did you read it all? Yes?

- Did you notice that the people in the account were in different difficulties at various phases in their lives?

- Did you notice that in each instance when they cried out for help, the Bible records that God delivered them out of their trials?

- So what makes us think that our situation is above God's ability to deliver?

- Whoever told us that God has given up on us?

The devil is a liar!

God is no respecter of persons. He will not do for those in Psalm 107 and not do for us.

- Let us not take God's promises lightly. Those promises are for us all. His promises are yea and amen! (2 Corinthians 1:20)

- He is willing, ready and more than able to fight for us His children.(Exodus 14:14)

- Let us always be cognizant of the truth that we have more going for us than going against us. (2 Kings 6:16)

- Greater is He that is in us that he that is in the world. (1 John 4:4)

- We have this assurance that the people who know their God will be strong and perform great exploits. (Daniel 11:32)

- We were promised that our latter would be greater.(Job 8:7)

We will not give up nor will we give in. We will get up and live out loud.

Let's pray

Our Father who art in Heaven hallowed be your name. Let your kingdom come, and your perfect will be done in me today. Thank you for always being my constant companion. Thank you for bringing me through every heartache, every hurt, every pain, and every strain. Thank you for your healing balm. In the dark season, in the night season, in every season, you are the light and the lifter up of my head. Thank you for lifting me up out of this distress right now. Great is your faithfulness to me Lord, and I thank you that your thoughts and intentions towards me are excellent. Help me to dwell my thoughts on those things that are honest, pure, just, lovely, of a good report and virtuous. In Jesus name. Amen.

Higher Altitudes: Lessons Learned at 35,000 ft.

LESSON #7

Regardless of our detours, we will get to our destination if we never stop short.

KEY NOTES:

- We must learn to push pass ourselves, to stretch ourselves, that's when growth takes place.

- We see and learn new things on our detours, however, detours are not destinations.

SCENARIO #7

Final Destination

It was not so long ago that I had the detour of my life. I was actually off for a few days using my rebated privileges to travel to the Zija Summit in Salt Lake City, Utah. Looking at the flight loads, I realized it would be impossible for me to go direct from New York, so I opted to travel through Washington, DC. It turned out that I would eventually have to travel through three other cities, before getting to Salt Lake.

The essence of this travel episode was that what should have taken me no more than four and a half hours, took me over twenty fourhours. I had to roll from flight to flight and go through three major cities before landing at my final destination.

My friend Michelle had gone ahead. She had quite similar circumstances out of Cincinnati but was already there for the commencement of the summit. Honestly, I felt like heading back home. I was tired, fatigued and at this point becoming most miserable. I would not, I could not be good company when I arrived. I definitely wouldn't want to hear anyone talking in my ear after all that. As the Lord would have it, I arrived late at night when all the ladies in our travelling party were sound asleep. I barely said hello to one who had heard me come in, bolted into the shower and went directly to bed. I was fresh and fine for breakfast the next morning, ready to enjoy the rest of the conference and the good company.

Yes – we all know, things in the natural are paralleled in the spiritual realm.

Truth be told – the Bible says:

Being confident of this, that he who began a good work in you will carry it on to completion until the day of Christ Jesus.
Philippians 1:6(NIV)

The fact of the matter is

I would have missed out on all the summit had to offer. I also would have forfeited the opportunity for excellent networking and the great fellowship we had during those few days, had I given up and returned home.

Have you ever had to fight through some stuff to get to where you wanted to be? I have fought some fights. It would take another book to tell you all about those.

But even when we felt like we couldn't move forward another inch, we found the strength by God's grace, to push pass ourselves to get the assignment completed.

When we have a task before us, when we have loved ones who depend on us, whenever we just have to move forward, we mustpull all our resolve to finish that project. When we have responsibilities to and for others, even a responsibility to ourselves, we must dig deep inside, put our shoulders up, fix our face forward and get to stepping.

We, my friends, are responsible for our actions. We sometimes cannot control the situation we find ourselves in, but we have total control over what we do and the decisions we make while in those situations.

I encourage us to look at our dreams, our goals, our desires, wants and needs as those projects that must be achieved. Let nothing – no slip nor fall, no knock down – let no one come between us and our dreams. Regardless of how much time we may have stood still or stayed on the ground, there comes a time when we have to start the ball rolling. Start from where we are and with what we have. And I am talking to myself as well.

Detours are only distractions. Delays were never meant to be denials. Disappointments teach us that the appointment we were hoping to have was never ours in the first place. It was not meant to be.

LIFE LESSON LEARNT?

Regardless of our detours, we will get to our destination if we never stop short…we must push pass ourselves…stretch yourselves…that's when growth takes place.

So what will it be?

1. Explain what is or was the biggest dream or desire for your life.

2. Have you arrived? If not, examine on a scale from one (1) to ten (10) how far off course have you detoured.

3. Identify those decisions you made in the past that caused you to steer off course.

4. Have you settled at your detoured location? If so, why?

5. How is your detoured location serving you now or how has it served you before? What lessons have you learnt that will allow you to avoid those same pitfalls?

So let's do this

Detours, delays, denials, disappointments – let us not disregard them, for they do have their purpose. They serve a greater purpose. They build strength of character. They teach us patience. They allow us to empathize with others, and when we would have matured pass those set of circumstances, it is then that we are prepared for the next level in our climb. It is by passing the test that we are promoted to the next class. The four (4) D's (detours, delays, denials, disappointments)should serve to propel us forward to our Final Destination.

Let's give ourselves permission to fall and fail sometimes. Falling and failing every time is a totally different story, but we're allowed to fall short sometimes and it's ok. It's quite human in fact. It's quite natural to become concerned when things do not turn out the way we planned. That now gives us another opportunity to work on some other solution. Out of every disaster comes an opportunity to learn something else. In the airline industry, it is after a malfunction or mishap of some sort that the authorities then sit down to review and revise that particular operation, and determine new methods of prevention and fail-proofing. We should handle our shortcomings in the very same way.

Remember we are not in this by ourselves. There's always someone just a phone call away willing and ready to help. And if for any reason you find yourself in a situation without someone to talk to, send us a private Facebook message on **Christian Arts and Empowerment Network** – we will get back to you. If your situation is outside of our scope, we'll be more than delighted to connect you with someone who has the expertise in handling your case. Above all, Jesus is just a prayer away.

I admonish us, let us use our setbacks as setups and step up to our higher altitude. Make every effort to move forward. Keep praying – keep pressing and keep moving forward. We have it in us to get past every hurdle. We owe it to ourselves to get to our final destination.

Let's pray

Father, you see all things, you know all things, and you care for me more than anyone else ever could. As I face these challenges, teach me the lesson you desire for me to learn. If I must go through this, if I must experience this, I will take comfort in the truth that you will never leave me nor forsake, but will be with me to the end. Give me the strength to keep moving forward when I don't feel like it. Let your joy be my power to press on to the mark of the high calling in you. I thank you that at the finishing line, I shall be able to look back and say that this was certainly the Lord's doing – it's marvelous in my eyes. I pray in the name of Jesus. Amen! Amen!! Amen!!!

Higher Altitudes: Lessons Learned at 35,000 ft.

THE DE-BRIEFING

So Let's De-Brief

So this is how this thing works.

There are four (4) forces that must be present for an aircraft to operate at its fullest capacity, and it is the pilot's responsibility to know exactly when and how to activate these forces. He or she either pulls a lever or pushes a button to engage and connect with any one of these forces.

These forces are:

- Thrust
- Lift
- Drag
- Weight

According to the simplest definitions from NASA (www.nasa.gov)

> **Thrust** is the force which moves an aircraft through the air. Thrust is used to overcome the drag of an airplane, and to overcome the weight of a rocket.

> **Lift** is the force that directly opposes the weight of an airplane and holds the airplane in the air.

Drag is the aerodynamic force that opposes an aircraft's motion through the air. Drag is generated by every part of the airplane (even the engines).

Weight is the force generated by the gravitational attraction of the earth on the airplane.

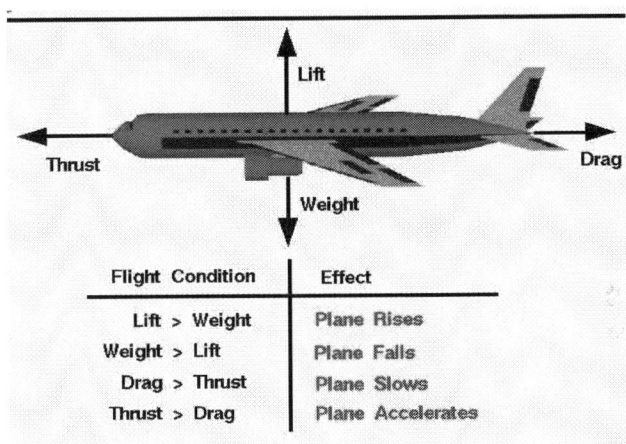

As with things natural, so are things spiritual.

As with the aircraft, our lives function with these same four (4) basic forces in operation around us. We must, therefore, be ever conscious of the fact that every action we take will either pull, push or propel us in one direction or another. Hence, our success (and everyone has their own definition of what success is for them) is qualified and quantified by our decisions. It is only fair that I remind us that not taking any action is still an action. It still is a decision.

In order to keep moving in the right direction, there are certain things that have to be in balance and must be measured ever so often, that we might verify our movement forward.

To ensure our progress forward and upward, our forces must be deliberately formulated in this fashion:

Lift > weight	=	upward motion
Thrust > drag	=	forward motion

On the other hand, we have to remember that:

Weight > lift	=	downward motion
Drag > thrust	=	backward motion
Weigh = lift	=	no motion
Thrust = drag	=	no motion

We have to cultivate an environment where we fashion our minds to fall in line so that our actions may be aligned. Where there is a strong will, we will find a way.

We must, henceforth, create for ourselves a list of our personal S.O.Ps, checks and balances that we employ to ensure that with time, we hit our target and arrive at our intended purpose.

Higher Altitudes: Lessons Learned at 35,000 ft.

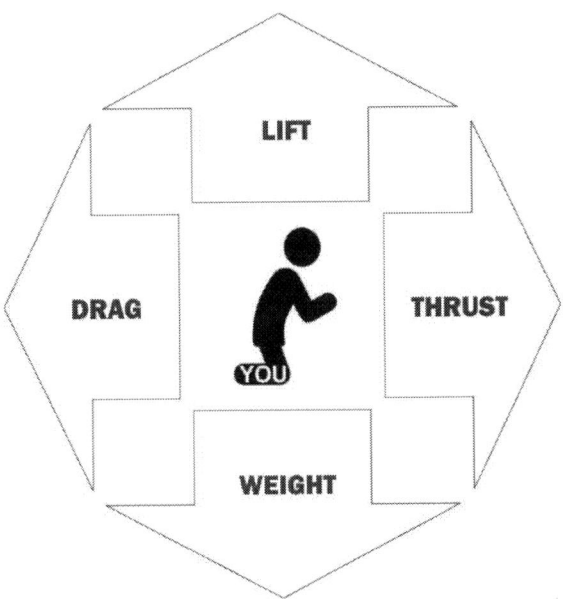

These physiological forces exist whether we feel them or not, whether we believe they do or not. Coupled with our decision to make prayer a prevalent part of our daily practice, the following diagram depicts the boost that is always derived from its consistency - from cultivating a lifestyle of prayer.

Higher Altitudes: Lessons Learned at 35,000 ft.

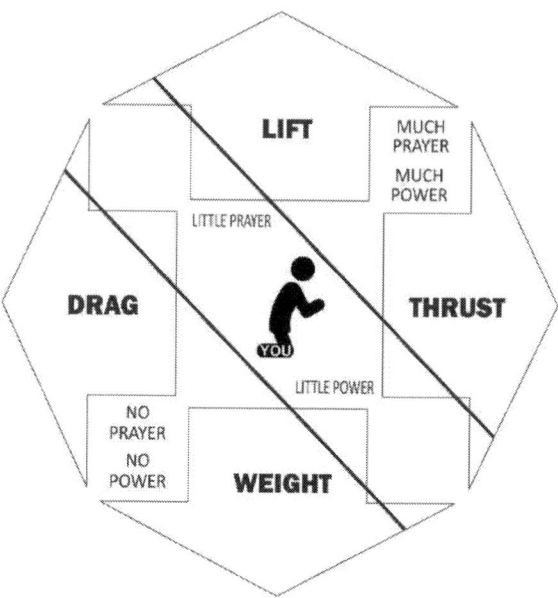

Did you notice that with **much prayer** our thrust and lift are prevalent? There is still some tendency to drag and weight, however, our movement forward and upward is dominant.

With **little prayer,** we are pretty much kept in a stagnant position, neither increasing nor decreasing much. This just allows us to maintain some kind of godliness, but there's not much power behind it. If being in the same place or same box every day all day is what you desire for yourself, then this will work for you, but as for me and my house, we need to forge forward – full blast.

With **no prayer,** we consistently find ourselves in the position of drag and weight. Things tend to pull us down a lot easier into a state of depression because we have not taken the time to create a cushion of communication with the Lord.

Please don't misunderstand me. Life does not become perfect when we pray. We will still have challenges and situations to deal with, however, we will definitely not be alone in our struggles. We will always have by our side, a *Senior Partner* – the *Chief Pilot* – to give us good, in fact, the best guidance ever. After all, the Holy Spirit is sent as the *Comforter* and as the One to guide us into all truth.

IN THE FINAL ANALYSIS

WHEN ALL IS SAID AND DONE

We are designed for progression. We keep moving forward while evolving mentally, emotionally, socially, and most important, spiritually. God is interested in seeing us grow and develop in every area of our lives.

As humans, we remember to develop our bodies by exercising. We concentrate on developing our minds by education, and these are all vital. However, we tend to forget that we are tri-part beings, and as such, pay less emphasis on the development of our spirit-man. This has been our weight and drag– our downfall. Because we as a people neglect to establish such a spiritual nexus with the Creator of Heaven and Earth, the Lord Jesus Christ, it hinders and limits us in the realm of that which is natural.

We must remember, Man is a spirit, possesses a soul and lives in a body. Every part of us needs to be cultured and developed to its fullest potential.

Know this -that the altitude we are living on right now, is not the level we were meant to settle on. We were called to live on a higher level. We were made for cruising at Higher Altitudes!

Little steps every day add up to giant shifts over time. We must take intentional steps and make deliberate decisions. We have to strategize with the conscious effort today, tomorrow, and every day, to make a difference in our own lives and in the lives of our neighbors - all those we come into contact with.

It is imperative that we learn to live daily with an attitude of gratitude. A little thankfulness goes a long way, and I am certain that we can find, without looking too hard, at least ten things to be thankful for.

We should surround ourselves with like-minded people. Make friends, cultivate relationships that propel us to a prosperous mindset. When our mind begins to conceive we will begin to receive wisdom and priceless ideas from the throne room of Heaven.

My friend, God wants for us to prosper and be in good health, mentally, emotionally, and spiritually. There is a purpose – a Higher Purpose – each of us was inimitably fashioned for. That assignment and calling that we must fulfil. We are uniquely designed for a reason.

We must seek out our Heavenly Father in prayer. We must allow Him to reveal to us our calling. When we begin to operate in our sphere, when we find our forte, and stay in prayer to the Lord Jesus Christ, then and only then will we begin to experience our Empowered Operative Position(E.O.P.) and enjoy our ***Higher Altitude.***

This is what the Bible says,

> *"Study this Book of Instruction continually. Meditate on it day and night, so you will be sure to obey everything written in it. Only then will you prosper and succeed in all you do".* Joshua 1:8 (NLT)

> *"Take delight in the LORD, and he will give you the desires of your heart"* Psalm 37:4(NIV)

Our most precious possession is our soul. Our most valuable gift is our gift of salvation bestowed to us by the One who gives 'good' gifts - Jesus Christ. He makes all the difference in our lives.

Remember this always:

> *"If you listen to these commands of the LORD your God that I am giving you today, and if you carefully obey them, the LORD will make you the head and not the tail, and you will always be on top and never at the bottom"* Deuteronomy 28:18 (NLT)

Before we go, do me this one favor, describe what you imagine yourself looking like if you were to live in consistency at your Empowered Operative Position (EOP) - at your Higher Altitude.

Write your own success story below.

Finish this paragraph:

When I live on my Higher Altitude, my life/relationship/marriage/career looks like:

_____

_____

_____

_____

_____

_____

_____

_____

_____

_____

_____

_____

My sister, my brother, we have it in us. Let's get up and take up our rightful position.

In the Final Analysis, we owe it to ourselves to live our lives on our **HIGHER ALTITUDE.** What would all this time spent here on earth be worth, if we just settled for less? Why not leave our mark, a legacy of prayer and power.

Let's climb...let's realize our fullest potential...we can do this...in Christ our **HIGHER ALTITUDE** awaits.

MY INVITATION TO YOU

It would be totally remiss of me if I did not do this.

I am extending an invitation to you, (if you are not yet saved and walking with the Lord, or if for some reason you walked away from the Lord) to accept the Lord Jesus Christ as your personal Lord and Savior. He is the 'best thing' that could ever happen to you. He will never leave you nor will He ever forsake you. He promises to be with you through thick and thin, once you are His child. He loves you more than you can ever love yourself.

> *"For this is how God loved the world: He gave his one and only Son, so that everyone who believes in him will not perish but have eternal life."* John 3:16(NLT)

So this is what I will ask of you, if you sincerely desire to live for Jesus. Believe in your heart and sincerely repeat the following prayer:

Father God, I come to you in the name of Jesus. I confess I am a sinner in need of your mercy and grace. Please forgive me of my sin and cleanse me from all unrighteousness. Create in me a clean heart and renew a right spirit in me. Wash me inside out with your precious blood. Be my Lord and Savior. Because I have asked from a sincere heart, I know you heard me and answered my prayer. I believe I am now saved – I am now your child and I will live for you daily with your help. Thank you, Jesus for your free gift of salvation. I receive it in Jesus' name. Amen.

Well, congratulations! And welcome to the family of Christ.

Now take steps to read and meditate daily on the Word of God. A good book to start with is the Book of John in the New Testament. Make sure to visit with a Bible Believing Church in your neighborhood. Let them know you just accepted Jesus as Lord and Savior.

I would also like to know how you are doing, so please drop me a message on our Facebook page – ***Christian Arts and Empowerment Network.*** I would love to pray with you and add you to our prayer list.

Blessings to you and all that you put your hands to, as you now begin to live at your **Higher Altitude**.

God's richest blessings.

Joanne

NOTES

Higher Altitudes: Lessons Learned at 35,000 ft.

Higher Altitudes: Lessons Learned at 35,000 ft.

About the Author

Joanne Harte has served in the airline industry for over thirty-five (35) years. She performed in various capacities – from Executive Assistant in the Human Resources Department to Flight Attendant, Flight Attendant Instructor and In-flight Director in the In-flight/Cabin Services Department.

Professionally, Hospitality and Protocol are her areas of expertise. If you asked her, however, she considers herself a 'forever student' of the Bible. She graduated Valedictorian and Best Class Debater from the Assemblies of God Bible Institute in Georgetown, Guyana, and continued her studies in Religious Education and Christian Counseling at Bible Institute & Seminary in Brooklyn New York.

Joanne has managed to masterfully merge her airline skills with that of her Religious Education, Christian Counseling and Biblical faith to now deliver lessons on living an empowered life at personalized Higher Altitudes.

Made in the USA
Middletown, DE
04 June 2019